BOOK ANALYSIS

Written by Flore Beaugendre
Translated by Jessica Foster

Lolita
by Vladimir Nabokov

VLADIMIR NABOKOV	**1**
American writer of Russian origin	
LOLITA	**2**
A scandalous novel	
SUMMARY	**3**
A childhood love that changed everything	
An all-consuming passion	
CHARACTER STUDY	**7**
Humbert Humbert	
Dolores Haze	
Charlotte Haze	
Clare Quilty	
ANALYSIS	**10**
The autobiographical form	
Rekindling the myth of Salome	
The influence of Lilith on Nabokov	
The posterity of *Lolita*	
FURTHER REFLECTION	**16**
Some questions to think about…	
FURTHER READING	**18**

VLADIMIR NABOKOV

AMERICAN WRITER OF RUSSIAN ORIGIN

- **Born in Saint Petersburg in 1899**
- **Died in Switzerland in 1977**
- **Notable works:**
  - *The Defence (1930)*, novel
  - *The Gift* (1937), novel
  - *Lolita* (1955), novel

Vladimir Nabokov was born in 1899 to an aristocratic Russian family. He was forced to leave his home country during the Russian Revolution and fled to Europe, where he began studying literature and wrote his first works. He notably published *The Defence* (1930) and *The Gift* (1937) which gained him recognition as a Russian-speaking writer.

Nabokov moved to the United States and acquired American citizenship in 1945. He refused to return to the USSR, and wrote in English. He became quite famous with this new audience. His fame exploded on a global scale in 1955 with the publication of *Lolita*. He subsequently published numerous novels. He died in France in 1977. He was a key writer of the 20th century.

LOLITA

A SCANDALOUS NOVEL

- **Genre:** novel
- **Reference edition:** Nabokov, V. (2000) *Lolita*. London: Penguin.
- **First edition:** 1955.
- **Themes:** passion, childhood, desire, revenge, jealousy, the myth of Salome.

Lolita is Nabokov's best-known work. It recounts the particularly ill-fated passion of Humbert, a man in his forties, for Dolores Haze, an American "nymphet" who is only just 13. A toned-down version of this plot can be found in *The Enchanter* (1939), which the author himself describes as "the first little throb of *Lolita*".

American publishing companies unanimously rejected it, and so the manuscript was published for the first time in Paris in 1955, as part of a collection of risqué and scandalous novels. Its publication caused a public scandal, with the book even being banned from circulation on several occasions.

SUMMARY

The book begins with a note from the editor, stating that the story is based on Humbert's manuscript. He tells us that the latter has died in prison, and that Lolita has also died. This intercession from a fictional editor aims to give a realistic, autobiographical dimension to the text.

A CHILDHOOD LOVE THAT CHANGED EVERYTHING

Humbert, the narrator, is a man of about 30. He describes his relations with women, which are dominated by his desire for young girls. In order to explain this attraction, he recalls his childhood in Europe and his "Annabel phase" (p. 8), his first love at the age of 13. He recounts the passion that united him with the little girl of his age and the shock of her sudden death. He sees this period of his life as the trigger for his future attraction to "nymphets", who have particular characteristics: a nymphet must be prepubescent, between 9 and 14 years old. Although she is graceful, she is not necessarily the prettiest little girl: it depends on the instinct of the narrator, the only one able to identify the "nymphic nature" (p. 10) of a young girl. These stages of his "pre-Lolita" past are glossed over. They are visibly there to give the reader the necessary means to gauge his character.

After his first marriage fails, he moves to America, where he falls into a depression. There he meets the Haze family, who are renting a room in Ramsdale, and describes his first glimpse of Lolita, lying in the 'piazza': "…and, from a mat in a pool of sun, half-naked, kneeling, turning about on her knees, there was my Riviera love peering at me over dark glasses" (p. 25). Gradually, we witness the beginning of a game of seduction, led childishly by Dolores, but satisfying the narrator.

From then on, he starts writing a diary in which he describes his all-consuming desire for the young girl, as well as his attempts to get closer to her, day after day. In passing, he also describes the mother of the prepubescent girl, Charlotte Haze, who he thinks is an annoying "old cat" (p. 31). But Humbert's excitement is interrupted when she announces that she wants to send her daughter away to a summer holiday camp. Shortly thereafter, Mrs Haze suddenly declares her love for him. Humbert is initially repulsed by the idea, but quickly sees the opportunity presented to him: to stay near his nymphet indefinitely ("I imagined [...] all the casual caresses her mother's husband would be able to lavish on his Lolita. I would hold her against me three times a day, every day", p. 46). He therefore agrees to marry Mrs Haze and becomes Lolita's father.

The diary then describes the fifty tiresome days spent in Charlotte Haze's company. The narrator's world collapses when his wife announces her decision to send Dolores to boarding school permanently: he is trapped. But an accident ends their cruel marriage: Mrs Haze finds her husband's diary. Devastated, she flees the house and is run over by a car. She dies, just as in Humbert's mad dreams. A new life begins.

AN ALL-CONSUMING PASSION

Humbert goes to fetch Dolores from camp, as her father. He tells her that her mother is ill and that they are going to see her in hospital. The little girl instantly begins her naïve game of seduction again. They spend the night in a hotel. It is then, according to Humbert, Lolita who marks a turning point in their relationship, which until now was innocent: "I had thought that months, perhaps years, would elapse before I dared to reveal myself to Dolores Haze; but by six she was wide awake, and by six fifteen we were technically lovers. I am going to tell you something very strange: it was she who seduced me" (p. 88). But Lolita is dejected and seems to understand and regret what has happened. The narrator also tells her of her mother's death. Consequently, he has become the only family she has.

The narrator recounts the endless journey, resembling an unending escape, that he makes with Lolita across America, from motels to bungalows, from arguments to forgiveness: "We had been everywhere. We had really seen nothing" (p. 115). A strained relationship is established between Humbert and Lolita, based on blackmail and lies. Humbert eventually decides to put an end to their journey, both in the hope of regaining a normal life and for financial reasons. They move to Beardsley where Lolita returns to private education. There she has drama lessons and appears in a play by the writer Quilty. She also tries to have more freedom, but the narrator refuses. Humbert, meanwhile, has found a job: he has become a university professor. But worries and jealousy gradually eat away at him. After yet another vicious argument, the young girl asks if they can go travelling again.

The pair embark on a journey, with Lolita defining the itinerary. Humbert soon notices that a man is following them and trying to make contact with the young girl. Lolita is playing both sides, but the narrator chooses to ignore it. When she falls ill and is hospitalised, however, in "fateful Elphinstone" (p. 163), she takes advantage of the opportunity to run away with a mysterious man, who turns out to be Quilty. She later admits to Humbert that he was the "only man she had ever been crazy about" (p. 181).

Humbert is deeply hurt and sets out to find her, enquiring in motels, where her abductor leaves mocking clues. Devastated, he ends up abandoning his mission. A year later, he meets Rita, who becomes his partner and a source of support: "[...] she was the most soothing, the most comprehending companion that I ever had, and certainly saved me from the madhouse" (p.172). Several years later, he receives a letter from Lolita: she is married, pregnant and wants money from her "dear Dad" (p. 177). He immediately goes to the address of the young woman and her husband, Dick. Dolores has no "nymphet" qualities now, but the love "at first sight, at last sight, at ever and ever sight" that she stirs in Humbert compels him to ask her to run away with him. She refuses, but does finally tell him about her disappearance with Quilty. We learn that he used her and abandoned her. Humbert is in shock. He goes to Quilty's house with a gun. Quilty is drunk and incoherent. The narrator subjects him to mental torture through a sort of symbolic trial, and avenges Lolita by executing him like an animal.

CHARACTER STUDY

HUMBERT HUMBERT

Humbert Humbert is both the narrator figure and the main character of *Lolita*. He was born in Paris in 1910. He represents the archetypal refined and cultured European: he is a private intellectual and a literature professor and specialist when it takes his fancy. His physical appearance is not described: we know that he is nothing special, but that he is seductive and successful with women.

Humbert is very mentally unstable – he is detained in a psychiatric ward twice. He is a liar and a manipulator, aware of his intellectual superiority. He does not bother with ordinary conventions and does not try to follow societal norms. His passion for Lolita is the centre of his existence, and outside of it he cannot establish social connections. In this way, he is perpetually out of sync with reality.

The relationship he had at the age of 13 is integral to the understanding of his character: "In point of fact, there might have been no Lolita at all had I not loved, one summer, a certain initial girl-child" (p. 5). His shock at the death of his beloved seems to have trapped him in that stage of his life; his obsession with young girls shows the quest for the love that he lost too soon.

DOLORES HAZE

Dolores was born in 1935. She was raised by her mother,

Charlotte, with whom she does not get on particularly well. She is 12 years old when the story begins. There are many descriptions of her physical appearance, all far-fetched, penned by Humbert. In his eyes, she is the true embodiment of the "nymphet". We learn that she is slender, with freckles and chestnut brown hair.

Lolita is a lively and impertinent young girl. Even in Humbert's opinion, she is not very intelligent, and is rather shallow. She is presented as the end result of the mass consumerist American society of the 1950s. In the novel, although she is visibly the instigator of the first romantic relations with the narrator, she is still an overwhelmed victim of the events. She is a naïve, lost orphan, and therefore an easy target for Humbert and Quilty. She never reaches the status of 'woman'.

CHARLOTTE HAZE

Charlotte Haze is the widow of Harold E. Haze, and has recently moved to Ramsdale. Although she is often described very negatively by Humbert, he admits that she is a beautiful woman, with noticeably intensified femininity. Like her daughter, Charlotte is slightly vulgar, not very cultured and not very quick-witted. The way the narrator describes her is, however, quite evidently unreliable, and the readers must gauge her character for themselves.

She is not often present and has a secondary role in the story, as we can see from the small amount of information that we learn about her. She is, however, an important figure in the work due to her relationship with her daughter. She is not at all lenient with Dolores and is jealous of her: she seems to view her more as a rival in her quest for Humbert's affection than as her daughter. She raises her to the rank of 'incomplete woman', which has many consequences.

CLARE QUILTY

Clare Quilty is an invisible, yet omnipresent, character. He is regularly mentioned, but always indirectly, whether being spoken of by the other characters or simply in the form of his voice ("I was about to move away when his voice addressed me", p. 84), right until his appearance in the final killing scene. Quilty's implicit presence makes him a threatening character. The allusions made about him scattered throughout the work are indications of his significance.

Clare Quilty is a moderately famous playwright and a decadent being. He could be viewed as his contemporary, Humbert's, double. They are both the same age, use the same type of language and they both lust after Lolita. Their final confrontation is therefore inevitable. By killing him, Humbert is, at the same time, punishing himself for his 'crimes', which are similar; only the punishment is different.

ANALYSIS

THE AUTOBIOGRAPHICAL FORM

Humbert, according to the fictitious John Ray, the supposed editor, would have called the manuscript *Lolita or the Confession of a White Widowed Male*. This title reminds us of the *Confessions* of Rousseau (French writer, 1712-1778), the pioneering work of the autobiographical genre, that we can see a parody of here. It is worth remembering also that Humbert is a specialist in French literature.

The narrator, in fact, subverts the rules of autobiography set out by Rousseau in his foreword: absolute sincerity, admission of sins and coherence, showing "all the integrity of nature". This is not the case in *Lolita* in which:

- Time is completely deconstructed: the story is formed of distortions and digressions, without concerning itself with the true duration of the events. Humbert does not respect the linear nature of his existence and shows in his approach that he only wants to recount what he finds interesting (Chapters 1-5).
- Humbert often expresses regret and despair towards Lolita's distress: "And there were times when I knew how you felt, and it was hell to know it, my little one. Lolita girl, brave Dolly Schiller" (p. 189). But these admissions are sporadic and often addressed to a sympathetic jury: "Gentlewomen of the jury! Bear with me!" (p.82).
His confession is marked by dishonesty, complacency and laborious justifications: "The stipulation of the Roman

law, according to which a girl may marry at twelve [...] is still preserved [...] in some of the United States" (p. 90); "it was she who seduced me" (p. 88). The character's sincerity is constantly called into doubt.
- We wonder whether Humbert is a reliable narrator. We know that he has psychological problems (he was hospitalised several times) and we know that he likes lying. He even declares his penchant for invention, which totally contradicts his claim that he is confessing.

  Thus, in this supposed biography, we can see a satire of the genre and of its inherent hypocrisy.

REKINDLING THE MYTH OF SALOME

Lolita can, for many reasons, be considered a modern version of the myth of Salome, recounted in the Gospel: Herodias' daughter, a young girl, is used by her mother to manipulate her husband, Herod. Herodias asks Salome to dance for him. Captivated by the beauty and appeal of his stepdaughter, he tells her that she can ask him for anything she wants. She demands the head of John the Baptist on a platter.

The narrative roles of the trio are the same in both cases, as the young girl seduces her stepfather before her mother's very eyes:

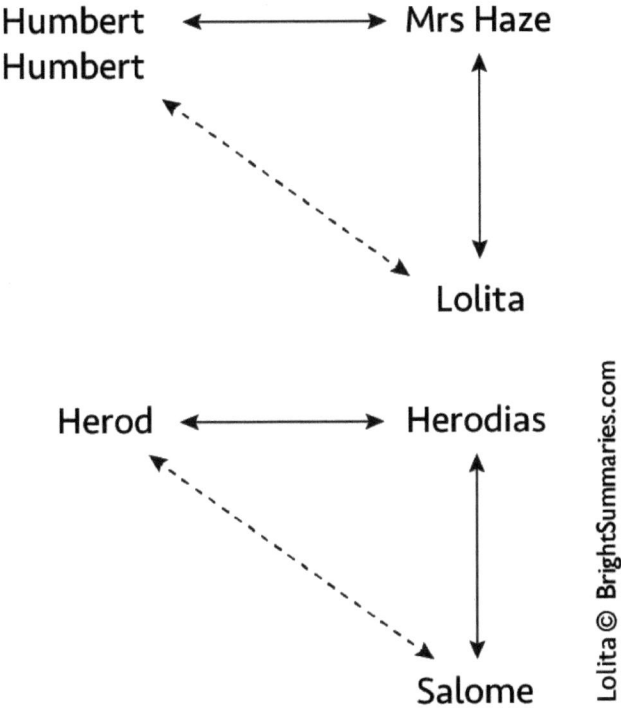

Salome's fatal power is in her youth and her grace, as well as in her sensual dancing. Dolores, on the other hand, is a "nymphet" who fascinates Humbert. He asks her to dance for him, after promising her various things. The comparison is therefore obvious:

> "On certain adventurous evenings, in Beardsley, I also had her dance for me with the promise of some treat or gift, and [...] the rhythms of her not quite nubile limbs had given me pleasure" (p. 152).

Salome is a synonym for destruction both for the prophet John the Baptist and for King Herod, who loses his free will and any control over his actions. The same is true of thoughtless Lolita who holds Humbert's destiny in his hands and prompts the death of Clare Quilty (as well as that of her own mother, indirectly).

Finally, Salome is defined as the "myth of perpetual combat between man and woman, flesh and spirit, irrationality and intellect"[1](Brunel, 1988). This could also apply to the relations between Humbert and Lolita, or, more generally, to Humbert's relations with women.

THE INFLUENCE OF LILITH ON NABOKOV

Lolita, the nickname chosen by Humbert, draws an obvious phonetic comparison with Lilith. Nabokov makes this link clear in this phrase: "Humbert was perfectly capable of intercourse with Eve, but it was Lilith he longed for" (p. 12). The poem entitled 'Lilith' that he had written in 1928 shows that he was indeed familiar with the myth. In the poem, he introduces a young girl who is very similar to our modern heroine.

Lilith, according to Jewish tradition, was the first wife of

Adam, before he sent her away from earthly paradise. She then became a succubus (a demon who takes the form of a woman to seduce a man). She is an incarnation of a sexual demon, a femme fatale and a dominatrix.

Humbert repeatedly insists on the demonic side of his beloved, and of "nymphets" in general: "[...] their true nature which is not human, but nymphic (that is, demoniac)" (p. 10). In the same way as Lilith, Lolita refuses to be subjugated, betrays the man and flees, condemning him to hell. She symbolises the destruction and the devilish influence of woman.

Lilith is the antithesis of the archaic woman represented by gentle Eve, Adam's second wife, who is both a bride and a mother. Charlotte Haze represents the adult femininity that Humbert rejects in favour of Lolita. Lilith, on the other hand, represents the incomplete woman, rejecting traditional sexuality and procreation. Lolita plays the role of Lilith, the child that the man cannot marry because she possesses none of his attributes. The final illustration of this inability to be a woman can be seen in Dolores' death during childbirth, giving birth to a still-born daughter. Lilith does not reach the rank of Eve.

THE POSTERITY OF *LOLITA*

The word 'Lolita' is now a commonly used noun. We use it to describe a stereotypical young adolescent girl whose behaviour is out of sync with her real age. It would be too simplistic to say that this description corresponds to the original character, who is much more complex and ambiguous.

Nabokov's heroine has therefore been taken from the novel and has become a modern icon of her own. The character has escaped from her author.

The reasons for this exceptional success can largely be found in the context of the work's publication: *Lolita* was published in 1955, when consumerist society was booming in Europe, and particularly in the United States. Sébastien Hubier explains this phenomenon:

> "[The resourceful innocents] are initially compared with ancient mythical figures before becoming a modern myth themselves, one that is directly linked to the growth of the consumerist society and the eruption of popular culture. This is why they are so closely linked to the characteristics and the great conflicts of the latter [...]"[1] (Hubier, 2007).

Lolita is therefore a new figure of the child femme fatale, consistent with the reality of an evolving modern society: consumption as a way of life, the cult of youth and the body, etc. She represents all of these disruptions.

---

1. All quotations taken from the reference editions have been translated by BrightSummaries.com

FURTHER REFLECTION

SOME QUESTIONS TO THINK ABOUT...

- The novel calls upon certain clichés about the difference between old Europe and America. Which ones? How are they illustrated?
- What makes *Lolita* an unsettling novel? Comment on the following quotation: "[Humbert] is abnormal. [...] But how magically his singing violin can conjure up a tendresse, a compassion for Lolita that makes us entranced with the book while abhorring its author!" (p. 4).
- Nabokov stated: "... *Lolita* has no moral in tow. For me a work of fiction exists only insofar as it affords me what I shall bluntly call aesthetic bliss..." (p. 210). Comment on this.
- It is not the first time in literature's history that the main character of a novel has been morally contemptible. Give other examples.
- Are there elements of a crime novel in *Lolita*? Explain your answer.
- In your opinion, what is the true role of the mother in the plot of *Lolita*? Is her relationship with her daughter significant?
- How do you think Nabokov's novel would have been received if it had been published nowadays?
- Lolita, in becoming a common noun, has become a modern-day icon. Give some examples of reprises of characters or of the plot of Nabokov's novel in literature, cinema, music, etc.

*We want to hear from you!
Leave a comment on your online library
and share your favourite books on social media!*

FURTHER READING

REFERENCE EDITION

- Nabokov, V. (2000) *Lolita*. London: Penguin.

REFERENCE STUDIES

- Brunel, P. (1988) *Dictionnaire des mythes littéraires*. Paris: Editions du Rocher.
- Couturier, M. (2010) Foreword. In V. Nabokov, *Lolita*. Paris: Gallimard.
- Hubier, S. (2007) *Lolitas et petites madones perverses: émergence d'un mythe littéraire*. Dijon: EUD.

FILM ADAPTATIONS

- *Lolita*, a film by Stanley Kubrick, starring James Mason, Sue Lyon, Shelley Winters and Peter Sellers, 1962. The film's screenplay was originally written by Nabokov himself, but, in the end, Kubrick only used it as inspiration. Nabokov, however, claimed to be satisfied with the film. It stays faithful to the book, but gives a more important role to the character of Quilty, who is somewhat subsidiary in Nabokov's novel. Kubrick, on the other hand, puts Peter Sellers at the forefront of the film several times, right from the outset: he is also a less threatening character.
- *Lolita*, a film by Adrian Lyne, starring Jeremy Irons, Dominique Swain, Melanie Griffith, Frank Langella, 1997. This second film is more faithful to the novel, in that

it reduces Clare Quilty to a secondary character and focuses more on Humbert's past and on his first experiences with "nymphets". Lyne provides a more explicit version of the sexual relations between Humbert and Lolita, something that was impossible in the 1960s, as Kubrick's film was subject to censorship.

Bright ≡Summaries.com

More guides to rediscover your love of literature

www.brightsummaries.com

© BrightSummaries.com, 2016. All rights reserved.

www.brightsummaries.com

Ebook EAN: 9782806279606

Paperback EAN: 9782806283023

Legal Deposit: D/2016/12603/362

Cover: © Primento

Digital conception by Primento, the digital partner of publishers.